The Wine Cup

By Richard Berengarten

Selected Writings: Shearsman Editions
Vol. 1 *For the Living : Selected Longer Poems, 1965–2000*
Vol. 2 *The Manager*
Vol. 3 *The Blue Butterfly (Part 1, The Balkan Trilogy)*
Vol. 4 *In a Time of Drought (Part 2, The Balkan Trilogy)*
Vol. 5 *Under Balkan Light (Part 3, The Balkan Trilogy)*
Vol. 6 *Manual: the first hundred*
Vol. 7 *Notness: Metaphysical Sonnets*
Vol. 8 *Changing*
Vol. 9 *A Portrait in Inter-Views*
Vol. 10 *Balkan Spaces : Essays and Prose-Pieces (1) 1984–2020*

Other Poetry
The Return of Lazarus
The Easter Rising 1967
Double Flute
Avebury
Inhabitable Space
Some Poems, Illuminated by Frances Richards
Learning to Talk
Roots / Routes
Half of Nowhere
Against Perfection
Book With No Back Cover
Do vidjenja Danice (Goodbye Balkan Belle)
DYAD (with Will Hill)

Other Prose
Keys to Transformation: Ceri Richards and Dylan Thomas
Imagems (1)
Imagems (2)

As Editor
An Octave for Octavio Paz
Ceri Richards: Drawings to Poems by Dylan Thomas
Rivers of Life
In Visible Ink: Selected Poems, Roberto Sanesi, 1955–1979
Homage to Mandelstam
Out of Yugoslavia
For Angus
The Perfect Order: Selected Poems, Nasos Vayenas, 1974–2010
Idea and Act

The Wine Cup

Twenty-four Drinking Songs
for Tao Yuanming

Richard Berengarten

Shearsman Books

First published in the United Kingdom in 2022 by
Shearsman Books Ltd
PO Box 4239
Swindon
SN3 9FN

Shearsman Books Ltd Registered Office
30–31 St. James Place, Mangotsfield, Bristol BS16 9JB
(this address not for correspondence)

www.shearsman.com

ISBN 978-1-84861-850-3

ACKNOWLEDGEMENTS

Grateful thanks to the fifth International Festival of Poetry and Liquor,
Luzhou, China, for awarding the 'Excellence Prize for English Poetry'
2021 to three of these poems, and to the editors of *The Use of English*
(72/1) and *Voice and Verse* (54), Hong Kong, each of which published
six of these poems, the latter together with Chinese translations by
Chen Shangzhen. Poems from this chapbook have also appeared in *Pari
Perspectives* and online in *Cambridge Critique* and *Margutte*.

Special thanks to my wife Melanie Rein, Paul Derrick, Anthony
Rudolf and Carl Schmidt for their invaluable comments and suggestions
on several earlier drafts of these poems.

Thanks too to Yang Guohua for the photo of a white clay drinking
cup from the Northern and Southern Dynasties Period (420 to 589 CE),
which is the source of the front cover image by Arijana Mišić-Burns. In
his early days, Tao Yuanming (365? to 427 CE) might well have drunk
from a cup such as this, though after he retired from public life to live
(and drink) in rural seclusion – so the story goes, under the shade of five
willows – it's doubtful if he would have used quite so fancy a vessel.

Contents

Dark Blaze

The way that can be wayed is not the way of ways

How many of us find the way of ways
That has no name? There's one reply: *Who knows?*
I sip my wine and relish its dark blaze.

I pour another cup. How the light plays,
Changing across the sky in streaks and glows!
How many of us find the way of ways?

Tracking the rising moon through summer haze
After my work is done, as the light goes,
I sip my wine and relish its dark blaze.

Dissolve desire? Stop searching? Simply praise?
Another cup, perhaps, before repose?
How many of us find the way of ways?

See fireflies flicker in their damp arrays
Down by the brook. Longing for dreamtime grows.
I sip my wine and relish its dark blaze.

Dusk thickens and my eyesight ebbs and sways.
Forgetting is a way too, I suppose.
How many of us find the way of ways?
I sip my wine and relish its dark blaze.

I pass the gate

My gaze drifts over the west garden
Where the hibiscus blooms – brilliant red.

I pass the gate. The red hibiscus blooms.
Its flowers fold. Soon they will fade and fall.
Come, drink a cup. Fate calls us to our dooms.

Remember palaces? Tall-ceilinged rooms?
Rich ceremonies? The emperor's gilded hall?
I pass the gate. The red hibiscus blooms.

Remember those fine servants, squires and grooms
Attendant on us, scurrying to each call?
Come, drink a cup. Fate calls us to our dooms.

Our skulls will soon be planted deep in tombs
Where feasting ants and cockroaches will crawl.
I pass the gate. The red hibiscus blooms.

Autumn already? Bring rakes, spades, and brooms.
Sweep summer up till no speck's left at all.
Come, drink a cup. Fate calls us to our dooms.

Change weaves its webs on insubstantial looms.
But here is wine. For this the clay grew tall.
I pass the gate. The red hibiscus blooms.
Come, drink a cup. Fate calls us to our dooms.

Dusts

On, on, on! After a hundred years
Body and name alike will be forgotten.

Now this thatched cottage is my hermitage,
Following quiet woodland paths seems best.
Against oncoming night, why rant or rage?

When young I was half-blinded in a cage
Of city-dust and rubbish, hope-possessed.
Now this thatched cottage is my hermitage.

Seventy-five, and still I earn my wage
By piecemeal work, with scant let-up or rest.
Against oncoming night, why rant or rage?

What point is there in shouting, at my age?
I grin, breathe deep, walk by, like any guest.
Now this thatched cottage is my hermitage.

My heart beats on against its old ribcage.
To touch the moment passing, that's the test
Against oncoming night. Why rant or rage?

A hundred years – our fate and heritage.
Considering that, I'm nothing if not blessed.
Now this thatched cottage is my hermitage,
Against oncoming night, why rant or rage?

Come in

Behind the cross-beamed door
I cheer my neighbours up with a jug of wine.

Come in and close the cross-beamed wooden door.
Good conversation waits, though the wind blows.
We've a full jug. How could we ask for more?

I've fed the stove. I've swept the worn brick floor.
The house is snug and warm despite the snows.
Come in and close the cross-beamed wooden door.

Don't stand on ceremony please. Now sir,
Hats off. Let's warm your frozen ears and nose.
We've a full jug. How could we ask for more?

Though blizzards sweep across bleak steppe and moor
And winter's dark and cold, and nothing grows,
Come in and close the cross-beamed wooden door.

Here, madam, slippers. And to warm your core –
as well as chilly fingers and numb toes –
we've a full jug. How could we ask for more?

It's friends who make a house a home. Therefore,
To friendship is the toast I will propose.
Come in and close the cross-beamed wooden door.
We've a full jug. How could we ask for more?

Loosen your belt

A guest, a guest!
If we've got some wine, let's pour it out.

Loosen your belt and drink with me a little.
The board sits ready. Let's not hesitate.
There's plenty more inside the glazed clay bottle.

Come in, it's cold. Put on the copper kettle.
Here's fire, food, warmth. Here's wine. And cup and plate.
Loosen your belt and drink with me a little.

Take off your coat and hood, my friend, and settle
Close to the fire, and I'll stoke up the grate.
There's plenty more inside the glazed clay bottle.

Ma jong? Or chess? Let's both be on our mettle.
We still have time before Death calls *Check Mate*?
Loosen your belt and drink with me a little.

The fire's a peony. Every flame's a petal.
Neither's a thing Death can appropriate.
There's plenty more inside the glazed clay bottle.

Life is the wine, my friend. Though in fine fettle,
Our flimsy vessels fasten us to fate.
Loosen your belt and drink with me a little.
There's plenty more inside the glazed clay bottle.

Over the stream

I drink a bit, and all sensations blur.
A second cup. So who gives a toss about Heaven?
Isn't that Heaven – there, just around the corner?

Over the stream, the gnats of summer dance –
An insect cloud, a clustered mist of wings,
And that's the way things are, by change or chance.

Two drinks bring pleasure, not deliverance,
So pour two more, see what two doubles bring,
Over the stream, the gnats of summer dance.

Now, after four, the lies of circumstance
Stop clinging, and the whole of nature sings
And that's the way things are, by change or chance.

Never mind *wills* and *won'ts* or *shalls* and *shan'ts* –
After two precious more we're sloshed as kings.
Over the stream, the gnats of summer dance.

Past six, the lives of men, insects and plants
Merge with the One *and* the Ten Thousand Things,
And that's the way things are, by change or chance.

So is it fate, old friend, or happenstance,
We stretch here – singing – plucking fortune's strings?
Over the stream, the gnats of summer dance
And that's the way things are, by change or chance.

Under the camphor laurel

Autumn. Brightness – doubled.
The camphor laurel, high as the high gate,
Has blossomed twice this year.

Come sit with me under the camphor-laurel.
Let creatures mate, breed, flourish and abound.
Open another cask, unplug the barrel.

Everything makes me thirsty. I'm in peril.
Let liquor pour. I love its gurgling sound.
Come sit with me under the camphor-laurel.

Vole, rat, hare, rabbit, badger, mouse and squirrel
Need drink – like us. So pour another round.
Open another cask, unplug the barrel.

The way to deal with things isn't to quarrel.
Sorrows are best dispersed by being drowned.
Come sit with me under the camphor-laurel.

You'll sing or hum some tune – folk song or carol.
I'll strum my lute. Who cares quite how we sound.
Open another cask, unplug the barrel.

Who says that drinking's wasteful or immoral.
Things feel much better once a drink's been downed.
Come sit with me under the camphor-laurel
Open another cask, unplug the barrel.

The evening star

Hey, we've got a guitar. So let's have a song.
Once we're sozzled we can totter off home.

You sang old songs. I strummed on a guitar.
We reminisced. We mixed up fact and fable.
We drank all day. Out came the evening star.

You brought wine in a round-lipped clay-glazed jar.
I asked you in. Your jar sat on the table.
You sang old songs. I strummed on a guitar.

We bantered – how things were and how they are,
Friendship our knot and wine its plaited cable.
We drank all day. Out came the evening star.

We solved the world. Our talk got circular.
We fell about, increasingly unstable.
You sang old songs. I strummed on a guitar.

You tottered home, which wasn't very far.
I sat and watched gnats clouding the west gable
We drank all day. Out came the evening star.

Who could compare with this? What silk-clad Czar?
What Emperor of Zhou? What Queen of Babel?
We sang old songs. I strummed on a guitar.
We drank all day. Out came the evening star.

Rivers and hills

Our feelings can reach farther than ten thousand miles
But our bodies are barred by rivers and hills.

I'm barred by rivers and I'm blocked by hills
All I wanted dissolves. As for desire,
things pass the way streams thread through watermills.

The nightingale is back. What singing skills –
Incessant song that never seems to tire.
I'm barred by rivers and I'm blocked by hills

Fine-tuned, my earthbound soul wells up and fills
With song – encompassed, satisfied, entire.
Things pass the way streams thread through watermills.

But I've heard eerier sounds at window sills
By night out there, receding further, higher.
I'm barred by rivers and I'm blocked by hills

Bring liquor now. And take care no drop spills.
Then pour – so we can all join in the choir.
Things pass the way streams thread through watermills.

Our candle flickers but the wick instils
Its blue blade through the yellow heart of fire.
I'm barred by rivers and I'm blocked by hills.
Things pass the way streams thread through watermills.

Empty house

It's desolate inside the empty house.
How could my cousin leave the world before me?

I drink alone, half-sleeping, half-awake,
Billowed by half-thoughts I can hardly bear.
Old friend, I'm just a ripple in your wake.

Just yesterday I rowed across the lake
To have a drink with you. Now in despair
I drink alone, half-sleeping, half-awake.

It's spring again. Ice melts. Flood waters break.
I'd packed a jar of wine for us to share.
Old friend, I'm just a ripple in your wake.

A plump bird flitted past. A coot or crake?
I knocked. Nobody opened. You weren't there.
I drink alone, half-sleeping, half-awake.

Was that house yours? My dream? Or my mistake?
Dust filled the place. Its cobwebbed cupboards bare.
Old friend, I'm just a ripple in your wake.

You've vanished like the dawn into daybreak
And haven't left a shadow anywhere.
I drink alone, half-sleeping, half-awake.
Old friend, I'm just a ripple in your wake.

Around my gate

I glance at my screen of trees. I keep the gate closed.
How long does anybody lodge in this cosmos?

Around my gate grow healthy plums and willows
Thrusting out blossoms. See how fast they've grown!
All winter long I've mourned lost drinking fellows.

Their ghosts entwine me and my spirit follows.
The geese return but my best friends have flown.
Around my gate grow healthy plums and willows.

My mind has lost its depths. I waste in shallows.
The best are shrunk to memory and bone.
All winter long I've mourned lost drinking fellows.

What is this moping fool that shrinks and wallows
Into decline and gloom and drinks alone?
Around my gate grow healthy plums and willows.

Give him a couch padded with extra pillows.
Who cares now if he wastes here on his own?
All winter long I've mourned lost drinking fellows.

Sleep, float him on your peaceful rippling billows.
He's drunk again. Forgive this rambling tone.
Around my gate grow healthy plums and willows.
All winter long I've mourned lost drinking fellows.

White

My flesh, shrivelling. Creased, my pallid face.
I can't believe how much white there is in my hair.

I've long relinquished any other goal
But getting by and living in the now.
My life isn't immortal. But it's whole.

I wield my sickle, net the leaping shoal,
I sow, prick seedlings, weed, hoe, prune and plough.
I've long relinquished any other goal.

Sometimes I wonder if the human soul
Moults shards or skins – and if it does so, how.
My life isn't immortal. But it's whole.

To live, then leave – a simple enough role.
Wiping the sweat off cheeks and furrowed brow,
I've long relinquished any other goal.

Look at my hair, snow-streaked. White takes its toll.
By evening, my shoulders droop and bow.
My life isn't immortal. But it's whole.

Wine helps. So, friend, let's ladle out a bowl
And smile at life a little anyhow.
I've long relinquished any other goal.
My life isn't immortal. But it's whole.

Scattered, my books

Poems and books pile up beside my chair
But the light's going. I won't have time to read them

Scattered, my books and brushes lie around.
I'm wide awake. I haven't slept a wink.
A misty night outside. No squeak. No sound.

My neighbours sleep. Most creatures go to ground.
But now the immortals wake. They prowl and slink.
Scattered, my books and brushes lie around.

My candle dims. Primeval fears abound.
How can I read or write, or even think?
A misty night outside. No squeak. No sound.

Shall I go mad? Heart drums and temples pound.
The dead awaken. Ghosts rise to the brink.
Scattered, my books and brushes lie around

Better this aching sleeplessness were drowned
In wine. I'm desperate for a drink.
A misty night outside. No squeak. No sound.

Appeased, my ghosts fall back in their profound
Tunnels and holes, where they collapse and shrink.
Scattered, my books and brushes lie around
A misty night outside. No squeak. No sound.

The long-winged cranes

My cloud-soaring cranes have stupendous wings.
In an eyeblink they're back, from the world's far corners.

The long-winged cranes fly by. Who knows where to.
I wonder where eventually they'll die.
Like us, they pass. Pass by, pass on, pass through.

Raising a glass, dear friends, I drink to you
Buried beneath the sorghum and the rye.
The long-winged cranes fly by. Who knows where to.

Bands of wild angels, how they whoop and mew!
Like aerial wolves, they howl. Like ghosts, they cry.
Like us, they pass. Pass by, pass on, pass through.

Passion is but a flower. It drinks in dew.
Love loves to drink but withers when it's dry.
The long-winged cranes fly by. Who knows where to.

When they have settled amid tall bamboo
will they breed there, these wind-blown Samurai?
Like us, they pass. Pass by, pass on, pass through.

Come out, dead friends, and drink. Against vast blue,
what silhouetted forms criss-cross the sky!
The long-winged cranes fly by. Who knows where to.
Like us, they pass. Pass by, pass on, pass through.

Hills and mountains

High mountains swallow my shadow
But my heart is truly not a stone.

Shadows of hills and mountains steal my own
And swallow it with minimal delay.
But I've a heart. I'm not a rolling stone.

Autumn again. This garden's overgrown,
And though light drenches everything by day,
Shadows of hills and mountains steal my own.

Come evening, before the sun climbs down,
my shadow lengthens, blurs, and melts in grey.
But I've a heart. I'm not a rolling stone.

As if dusk clutched me in long arms, breeze-blown,
And coddled me, protectively, in play,
Shadows of hills and mountains steal my own.

When cloudy night, black-robed, ascends her throne
She'll squeeze my shadow till it drains away.
But I've a heart. I'm not a rolling stone.

I'll be engulfed soon – breath, flesh, entrails, bone –
A creature fashioned out of mud and clay.
Shadows of hills and mountains steal my own,
But I've a heart. I'm not a rolling stone.

Chrysanthemums

Autumn chrysanthemums! What gorgeous colours!
I pluck their flowers, dew-wet. Then float them
On the surface of this – whatsit – that drowns care.

Whatever is, has form. What's born becomes
Death-fruit – death being birth's corollary.
Autumn is back with gold chrysanthemums.

Everything's ripened – apples, damsons, plums,
I've picked them, twisting each stem carefully.
Whatever is, has form. What's born becomes.

I've rubbed skin-bloom off fingers, licked my thumbs,
Sucked juices out. Such sensuality!
Autumn is back with gold chrysanthemums.

I'm still in rapture. Consciousness succumbs
To this abundant prodigality.
Whatever is, has form. What's born becomes.

I still hear bee-hordes. My whole being thrums.
I pick flower-heads to dry for wine and tea.
Autumn is back with gold chrysanthemums.

Blackbirds peck berries. Sparrows, fallen crumbs.
And me? Drunk without drinking, on a spree.
Whatever is, has form. What's born, becomes.
Autumn is back with gold chrysanthemums.

First Frost

Dew freezes. No mists drift.
Pungent chrysanthemums blaze, open up the woods.
A line of green pines crowns the cliffs.

A crispness on the air, a chill, first frost,
Pines silhouetted on the sheer cliff-top,
Chrysanthemums ablaze in petalled rust.

Here is completeness, no waste, nothing lost,
Between what's far and near, no chasm or gap,
A crispness on the air, a chill, first frost.

Chill flames bloom with an acrid tang of must,
Searing the wood's edge, petal-frills knife-sharp,
Chrysanthemums ablaze in petalled rust.

While past the pines, in lines of mauve, criss-crossed,
The mountains' chorus quivers like a harp.
A crispness on the air, a chill, first frost.

However pressed, expressed, impressed, compressed,
This natural music keeps perpetual shape –
Chrysanthemums ablaze in petalled rust.

A man may be a ghost pressed out of dust
But me? I'm drunk and haven't touched a drop.
A crispness on the air. A chill, first frost.
Chrysanthemums ablaze in petalled rust.

Pines

Snow fell all day long, shrouding everything
Cold, the wind at year-end.

Huge pines, like marshalled ghosts, stand robed in snow,
Ranging the hillside, silent sentinels
Guarding my thatched ramshackle bungalow.

Our ancestors three thousand years ago
Read futures from ox-bones and turtle-shells.
Huge pines, like marshalled ghosts, stand robed in snow.

Do trees enshrine their spirits? Who would know
What inner secrets *Change* holds or foretells,
Guarding my thatched ramshackle bungalow?

Late winter. Now the sky's deep indigo
Turns blue, then black. In sombre aquarelles
Huge pines, like marshalled ghosts, stand robed in snow.

Each to its pattern. Nothing can forego
Its form, *just-so*, fine-spun in frost-fixed spells
Guarding my thatched ramshackle bungalow.

Come, have a drink. There's nowhere else to go.
Forget your sorrows. Wine warms and dispels.
Huge pines, like marshalled ghosts, stand robed in snow
Guarding my thatched ramshackle bungalow.

Ends

The empty boat drifts off. No oar directs it.
To being human there's most definitely an end.

The end is where things stop. It's not a thing.
But rather a *no*-thing, an emptiness.
Once it arrives, there's no more numbering,

No scurrying, no self-encumbering,
No counting out or down, no *more* or *less* –
The end is where things stop. It's not a thing.

No *other* and no *else*, no square or ring,
No angle, line or curve, no strife or stress –
Once it arrives, there's no more numbering.

Nothing to take away, nothing to bring,
No time, no tense, no map, no fixed address –
The end is where things stop. It's not a thing.

So sit down, friend, and drink. Stop worrying.
We're not there yet and worry's meaningless.
Once it arrives, there's no more numbering.

And who knows what this evening may bring?
Tears? Wonder? Visions? Peace? Forgetfulness?
The end is where things stop. It's not a thing.
Once it arrives, there's no more numbering.

Four maples

Once the door of the dark house closes,
For a thousand years, no more morning.

Four maples frame the house. Elms shade the fence.
A temple, maybe? Could it be a shrine?
I can't make out it its full circumference.

Is this a guesthouse? Someone's residence?
A voice responds, *It's neither yours nor mine.*
Four maples frame the house. Elms shade the fence.

What brought us here? Mere chance? Fate? Providence?
And is its purpose suspect or benign?
I can't make out it its full circumference.

How have our paths merged here, in confluence?
The way seemed simple but I saw no sign.
Four maples frame the house. Elms shade the fence.

Couldn't we pause here? Might a drink make sense?
I wouldn't say no to a cup of wine.
I can't make out it its full circumference.

Mightn't these clusters of coincidence
Mark undercurrents that we can't define?
Four maples frame the house. Elms shade the fence.
I can't make out it its full circumference.

The poets' wine-shop

While the white stones of Needle Island glisten,
Not a single cloud looms over Mount South.

Between skies of pure azure and sea blue
The poets' paradisal wine-shop stands
Inside the gate that lets newcomers through –

Isn't this wine-shop waiting for you too
By the last harbour, past time's drifting sands,
Between skies of pure azure and sea blue?

Come, sit down, watch the dancers, drink the brew
And listen to the best performing bands
Inside the gate that lets newcomers through

And cast off evening shade and morning dew
For here eternal timelessness expands
between skies of pure azure and sea blue.

And see who's here! Wang Wei, Li Bai, Du Fu
Tao Qian – all rise to greet you. Come, shake hands,
Inside the gate that lets newcomers through.

See Mount Penglai rise high above Daiyu
Misted among the lost immortal islands
Between skies of pure azure and sea blue
Inside the gate that lets newcomers through.

Whatever comes

My garden's littered
With fallen leaves. Autumn.

Whatever comes, comes of itself, just-so.
Things whisper. See, *this-now* is *such-and-such*.
What makes things this way who'll ever know.

Lengthening silent shadows loom. They throw
Cloaks over hills without seam, trim or stitch.
Whatever comes, comes of itself, just-so.

The frozen carp-pond casts an eerie glow
Back at the moon. I lift my wooden latch.
What makes things this way who will ever know.

I tread outside. My footsteps crunch fresh snow.
Change – that's the one fish nobody can catch.
Whatever comes, comes of itself, just-so.

I'll warm a jug over my wood-stove's glow
Despite the draught that mutters through my thatch.
What makes things this way, who will ever know.

I relish small sips, take my drinking slow.
I may know some things, but not very much.
Whatever comes, comes of itself, just-so.
What makes things this way, who will ever know.

A hundred years?

Humans lease a body for up to a hundred years
But end up in the twinkling of an eye.

We lodge here for at most a hundred years
Then perish in the twinkling of an eye.
That's just the way things are. No cause for tears.

Life moves in subtle interlocking spheres.
You get your turn at it and so do I.
We lodge here for at most a hundred years.

Your death's a window through which *Nothing* leers
With eerie eyeless grin. Don't grieve. Don't sigh.
That's just the way things are. No cause for tears.

No summer sky can bring effective cures
For winter, which must enter by and by.
We lodge here for at most a hundred years.

What should we do then to allay our fears
Of *Nothing*? Nothing! Does your throat feel dry?
That's just the way things are. No cause for tears.

So, bottoms up! We may as well get by
By drowning fear – and spitting in Death's eye.
We lodge here for at most a hundred years
That's just the way things are. No cause for tears.

Until this liquor drains

I've a fine wine here. Let's share it.
A crane calls in the shade. Its chick answers.

Ineffable the ways the Way remains,
Unspoken, all-enduring, never-ending.
Love, drink with me until this liquor drains.

And pity the self-hater who abstains,
Refraining from desire, stiff and unbending.
Ineffable the ways the Way remains.

Ingredients of fruits, herbs, berries, grains –
What inner fire resides in their fine blending.
Love, drink with me until this liquor drains.

Its tastes – so complex! How the mouth retains
Echoes of subtle flavours, time-suspending.
Ineffable the ways the way remains.

Threading through tunnelled arteries and veins
Its fire fans out, ever itself-extending.
Love, drink with me until this liquor drains.

Come, sit outside with me and watch the cranes
Fly overhead. Heart-warming? Or heart-rending?
Ineffable the ways the way remains.
Love, drink with me until this liquor drains.

Postscript

In February 2019, an unexpected invitation arrived from the Luzhou Laojiao Distillery in Sichuan, to write some poems on the theme of, "poetry and liquor". At that time I happened to be reading some English translations of poems by Tao Yuanming (365–427 CE). As soon as the invitation arrived, an idea struck me. I started writing straight away, and relatively effortlessly and spontaneously a set of twenty-four poems flowed from my pen. During composition, at times it even seemed that Tao Yuanming was sitting beside me, that his voice was echoing in my head, and that through these incipient new poems in English, this voice was telling me exactly how they wanted to be written and what needed to be said. All I needed do was accept and follow this voice, at once intimately familiar and strangely *other*.

Among the many things I love about Tao Yuanming are his vulnerable humanness and his Daoism. To me these are inseparable. I dedicate *The Wine Cup* to his immortal memory, hoping this homage will clarify and endorse my belief that this *miglior fabbro* and wise, gentle man is a great and noble Lord of Poems and, equally, a great and noble Lord of Wine.

❧

Most of these poems have an epigraph that I've rendered into English from Tao Yuanming, sometimes as a collage improvised from several texts. The first poem's epigraph is my version of the opening line of the *Dao De Jing*, with acknowledgements to A. C. Graham's translation. The epigraph to the final poem combines a quote from Tao Yuanming and from the *I Ching*.

All the poems are villanelles. This form creates a song-like pattern of rhyme and resonance that embodies and echoes the cyclic rhythms of nature. I believe the villanelle's structure reflects at least some aspects of the formality, economy and delicacy of Tao Yuanming's poems.

The two-volume bilingual Chinese-English text of Tao Yuanming I've relied on in making these poems is *T'ao Yuanming, His Works and their Meaning* by A. R. Davis (Hong Kong University Press, 1983, and Cambridge University Press, 2009). This translation delivers Tao's poems into English in a literal, modest and transparent way, without frills, affectation or adornment. A. R. Davis's erudite notes, glosses, questions and uncertainties make his versions all the more valuable.

Cambridge, August 2022

Dedications

'Dark blaze', p. 1. In memory of my cousin Paul Winner (1934–2019).

'I pass the gate', p. 2. For Robert (Jihui) Peng.

'Dusts', p. 3. For Richard J. Smith (Sima Fu).

'Come in', p. 4. For Yang Guohua, Xu Zhe, Yang Zizhen and Yang Ziying.

'Loosen your belt', p. 5. For Tan Chee Lay and Ng Lai Sze.

'Over the Stream', p. 6. For Chan Shangzhen and Guo Lan.

'Rivers and Hills', p. 9. For Tammy Ho Lai Ming.

'Empty house', p. 10. In memory of Paul Pines (1941–2018).

'White', p. 12. For Wu Jidong and Chen Dongni.

'The long-winged cranes', p. 14. For Hon Tze-ki.

'Hills and mountains', p. 15. For Yu Mingquan.

'Chrysanthemums', p. 16. For Catherine and Kenneth Ng (Lin Xueqing and Wu Jinyong).

'First frost', p.17. For Paul Scott Derrick.

'Four maples', p. 20. For Alan Trist.

'Whatever comes', p. 22. For Edward L. Shaughnessy (Xia Hanyi) and Elena Valussi (A Linna).

'A hundred years', p. 23. For Ren Qi.

'Until this liquor drains', p. 24. For my wife, Melanie Rein.

Biographical Note

RICHARD BERENGARTEN (Chinese name *Li Dao*, b. London 1943) is an English poet whose writings have been translated into more than 100 languages. His poetic mosaic *Changing* (2016), a homage to the *I Ching*, has been greeted as a leading contribution to the ongoing dialogue between ancient Chinese thought and 21st century poetry and poetics. RB's distinctions include PEN Slovenia *Guest-of-Honour* (2020), the *Xu Zhimo Silver Willow Award* (2017), the *Manada Prize* (Macedonia, 2011), Freeman of the City of Kragujevac (Serbia, 2010), *Poet-in-Residence*, Dante/Eliot Conference (Firenze, 2008), the *Morava Charter Prize* (Serbia, 2005), the *Jewish Quarterly-Wingate Award* (1992), *Yeats Club Prize* (1989), *Keats Poetry Prize* (1974), and an *Eric Gregory Award* (1972). RB has lived in Italy, Greece, the USA and former Yugoslavia, and has enjoyed visits to China, including international poetry events in Chengdu, Xichang, Luzhou and Gulangyu. In 1975, he founded the now-legendary international Cambridge Poetry Festival, and in 2015 he was one of the coordinators of the first Xu Zhimo Festival. He lives in Cambridge, where he is a Bye-Fellow at Downing College and an Academic Associate at Pembroke College. His voice and poems are recorded online on the *Poetry Archive*: https: //poetryarchive.org/.

Lightning Source UK Ltd.
Milton Keynes UK
UKHW011812100922
408646UK00001B/47